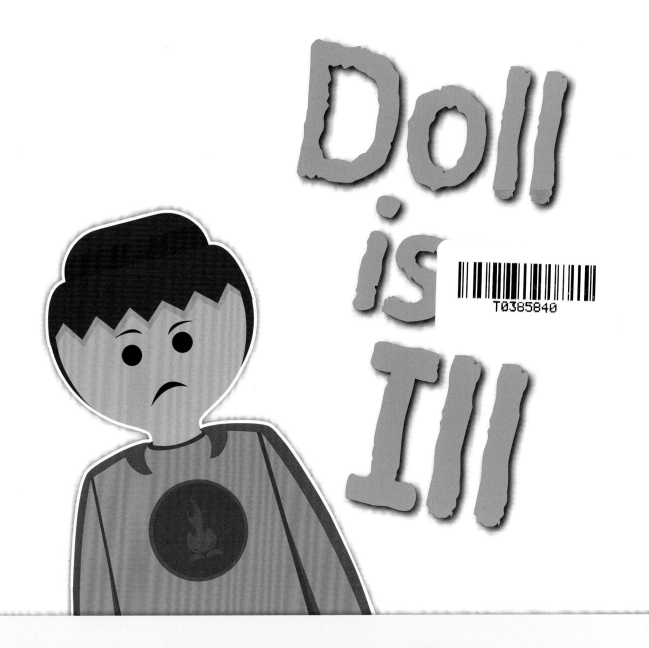

Doll is Ill

Written by Jeanne Willis

Illustrated by Rita Giannetti

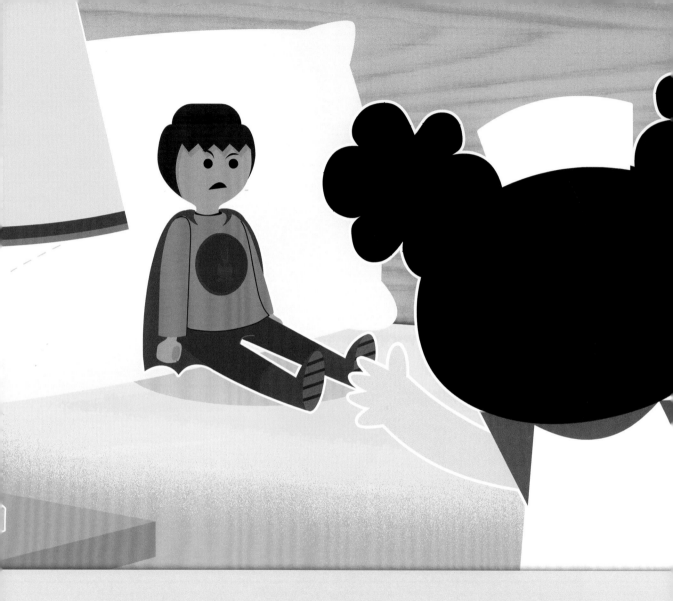

Doll is ill.
Bad luck, Doll!

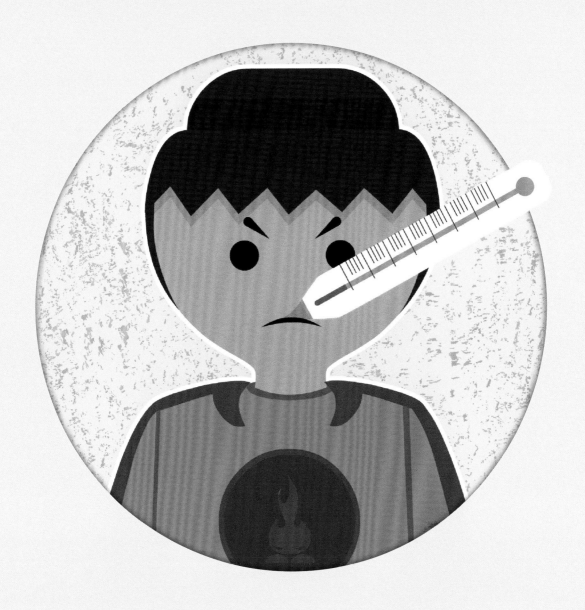

Doll is hot!

3

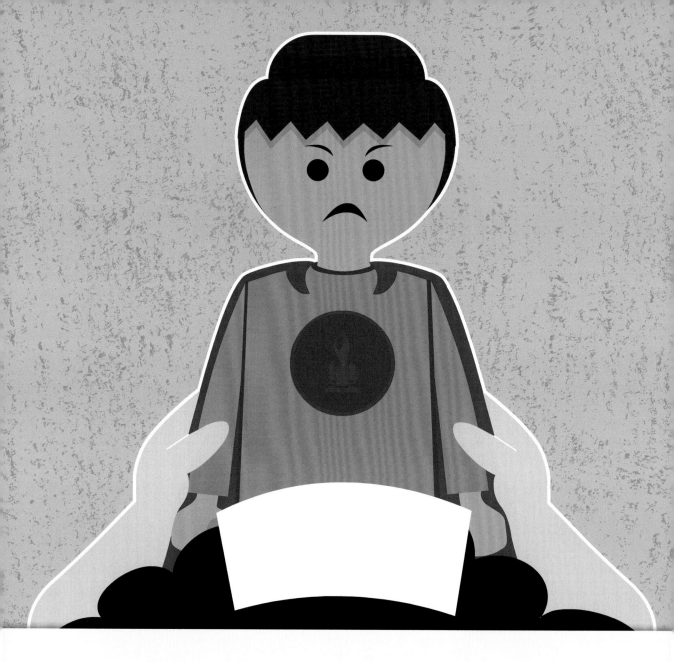

I bet Doll has a bug.

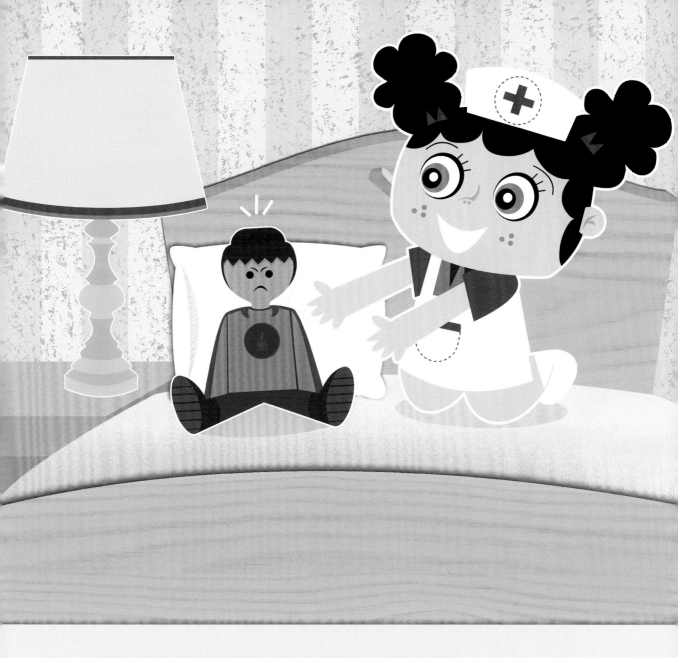

Get into bed, Doll.

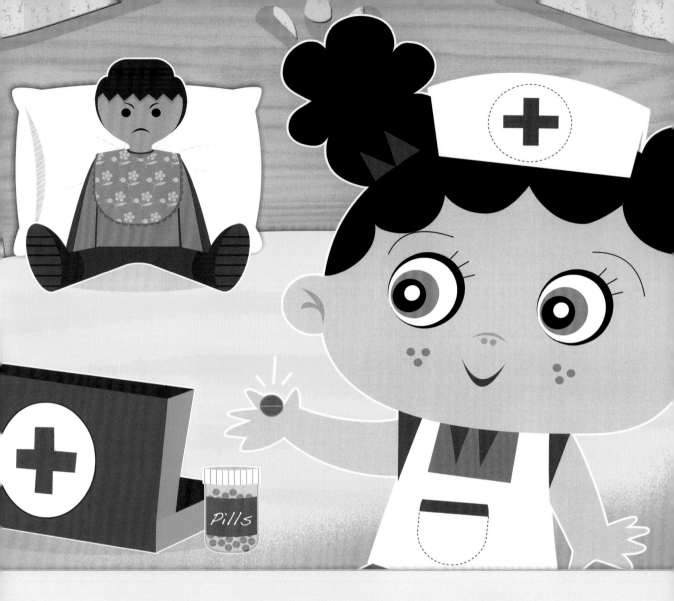

I can get Doll a pill.

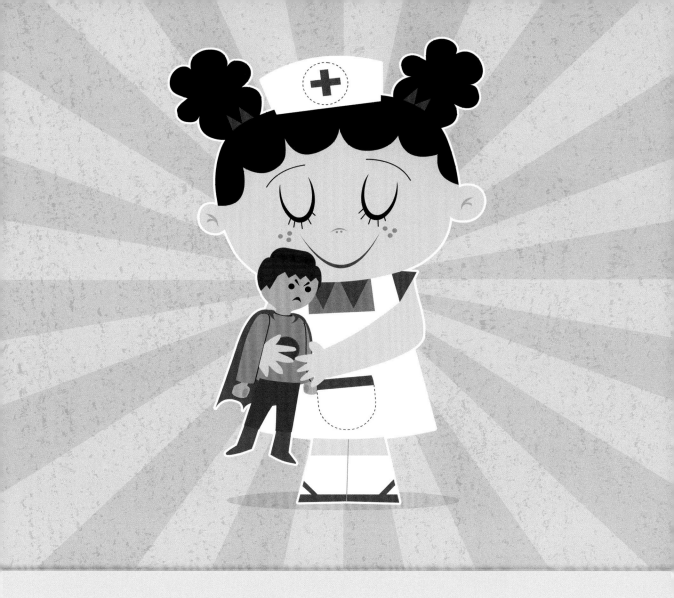

Kiss! Kiss!
Lots of hugs.

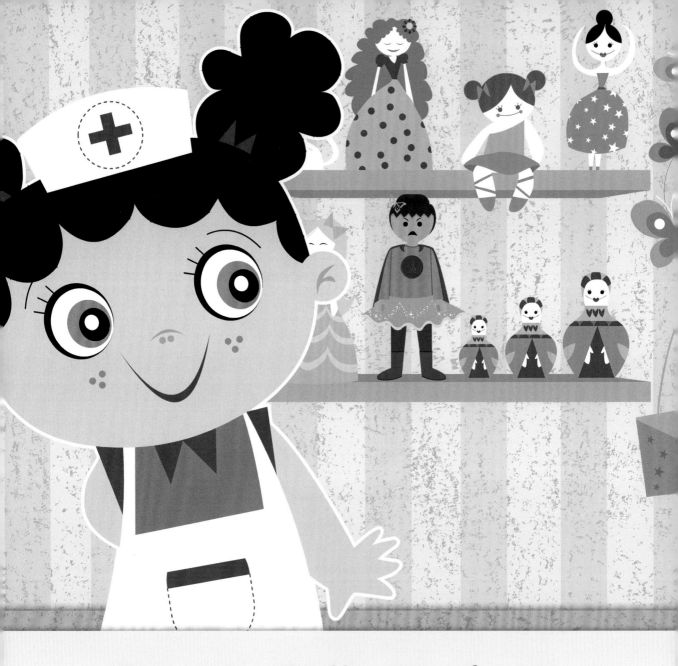

Get up, Doll! No fuss!